MW01281802

# Nine Changed Lives

Monologues For Lent and Holy Week
By Cynthia S. Baker

## C.S.S. Publishing Co.
Lima, Ohio

# NINE CHANGED LIVES

Reprinted in 2003

For more information about CSS Publishing Company resources, visit our website at www. csspub.com, email us at csr@csspub.com, or call (800) 241-4056.

ISBN-10: 1-55673-282-1
PRINTED IN USA

## DEDICATION

To my dear friends at Palo Congregational Church, for being backstage help, cast, and appreciative audience, this book is affectionately dedicated.

# TABLE OF CONTENTS

# INTRODUCTION

You can't make bricks without straw? If the "bricks" are dramatic productions, and the "straw" is the big budget, or ideal facilities, sometimes you can.

The churches I have been involved in have all been small, with limited facilities — no curtained stage, no sound equipment, no special lighting, no scenery flats. Our costumes have been simple; our casts have been enthusiastic but untrained. Yet I believe many of our productions have been very effective.

For more than 30 years, my husband and I have worked with young people, and many of my plays were written for them to perform. I wrote *Nine Changed Lives* because my husband wanted to have dramatic skits instead of a series of sermons for Lenten worship. We cast both teenagers and adults in the roles.

The series of nine skits begins with a bare cross at the front of the sanctuary. The cross remains through Easter. We chose symbols bearing on Easter, and I wrote a monologue (or dialogue) based on each one, using characters associated with them. After each drama, one of the players adds the new symbol to the cross, so that by Good Friday, the cross is covered with symbols. But on Easter morning, for the final presentation, the cross is empty again.

I believe the skits would be useful for any size church; but they are especially suitable for small ones.

**Cynthia S. Baker**

# FOREWORD

*Nine Changed Lives* the title says. It should say 10.

Our church used these plays two years ago. I am changed. Never again will I be able to read the story of Jesus' last days without thinking of the participants as real people. Cynthia Baker has taken the obvious and made me notice it.

I had not thought of how Simon of Cyrene could have felt as he carried the cross for Jesus. What about that centurion who said, "Surely this was the Son of God"? When he realized whom he had crucified, what happened to his life? We can only guess, but Cynthia's dialogues talk to us. They use Bible facts, yet lead us to ponder the hearts behind the names.

We hear Tamar, the maid who confronted Peter. She wonders why Peter cried so hard when the rooster crowed. We listen in as Claudia berates her husband, Pilate, for not heeding her warning.

A couple of years ago I watched a blue-eyed television Jesus as he angrily cleared the temple. Later he spoke words which today are so easily romanticized as oft-quoted memory verses. But that day, I was struck with reality: Jesus was a man. I know him as God, my personal Savior, Lord of my life. But there were people who saw him sneeze, who heard a seeming mere human say, "I am the bread of life." And they believed him. Why? Because he was real to them.

The book of Luke opens with ". . . it seemed good also to me to write an orderly account for you . . . so that you may know the certainty of the things you have been taught." These dramas give breath to those things.

In the Palm Sunday drama we hear one boy saying to another, "Come and see." On Easter Sunday Mary Magdalene urges the disciples, "Come and see." Isn't that also our goal? We want people to come to our churches and see Jesus. Then Jesus changes lives.

6

These nine brief skits, using few characters, sets or props, repeatedly turned my thoughts to Jesus. I invite you, too, to turn the page, and come and see.

**Solveig Swanson**

# SIMON OF CYRENE
Monologue For Ash Wednesday

**CHARACTER:** **Simon of Cyrene:** If possible, played by a black actor, with or without beard. He is wearing a simple tunic of some dark color with a robe over it, long-sleeved and unbelted.

**PROPERTIES:** A large wooden cross of rough wood, large enough so that a man might die on it. On the platform is a base into which the shaft of the cross fits, so that when Simon reaches the platform, he can stand the cross up. *(See diagram showing construction of cross and base.)*

**SCENERY:** None needed. A simple curtain across the back of the stage is effective. Skit is intended for use in a church sanctuary.

---

*(Enter Simon at rear of sanctuary, bearing a large wooden cross on his back. Slowly, and with obvious effort, he proceeds to the stage, crossing from right to left to place cross in cross base, stage left. He steps back to center stage, still looking at the cross. Then he turns toward the audience.)*

**SIMON:** Well, there it is — the cross. It really doesn't look like much, does it? Two pieces of wood, one across the other.

But like any other symbol, it's not what it **is** that's important. It's what it makes you think of.

*(He turns and paces to stage right, and back to center.)*

I'll tell you what it makes **me** think of. My name is Simon, from the city of Cyrene, in Africa. I'm a Jew. Like all other Jews who take their religion seriously, I've always gone to Jerusalem for the Passover, even though it's quite a trip there from Cyrene. I was there this year, too.

In fact, I had just arrived at the outskirts of the city when I was barred from going any farther by a procession of some sort, coming down the narrow street toward me. I saw the soldiers, and I got out of the way, well over to the side. You don't pick a fight with Roman soldiers, not if you're smart. *(He moves to the side, stage right.)*

When they got a little closer, I was sickened to see that it was a group of three men carrying their own crosses, obviously on their way to their own execution, and guarded by a Roman squad. I wanted nothing so much as to get out of there, but the crowd was so dense I couldn't move.

Then, to make everything worse, one of the three men stumbled and fell under the weight of his cross, right in front of me.

*(He pauses and looks down in front of him, as if he could still see the body.)*

I could see his back, and it was a mass of bleeding welts; he had been severely scourged. It was no wonder he couldn't get up. One of the soldiers yelled at him and kicked him but the centurion stopped him, and began looking over in my direction. It was my misfortune to be the biggest man in the crowd. He called me out, and I went — not willingly, but because he had a sword, and the power of Rome on his side.

*(He moved back to center stage.)*

"Give us a hand with this cross, fellow," he said. They lifted the cross up off the fallen man, and laid it on my shoulders, and then they yanked him to his feet. I wanted no part of helping them with their dirty work — but suddenly, the man who had fallen turned his head and looked straight into my eyes. That look was like a sword going through me, and I

10

remember thinking, "I won't do it for **them** — but I'll do it for you, whoever you are."

So I carried the cross out of the city to Calvary, walking in the midst of the soldiers and the crowd, along with those men who were doomed to die.

*(He walks over to the cross, and puts his hand on it.)*

It was a cross like this — a symbol for the cruelest of deaths, of shame, of disgrace reserved for the worst of criminals. All the way, as we went, I wondered about the man who had been carrying it. That look in his eyes told me he was no criminal.

*(He walks to center stage, moving closer to the front.)*

Well, you know what they did to him that day, on the cross. I couldn't rest after that until I found out more about him. Now I know who Jesus of Nazareth was, and who he is. I thought **I** was doing something for **him** that day, but it turns out he was doing something for **me**. He was suffering on this cross, and dying on it, for me. When I understood that, it made a disciple out of me.

He died for you, too, that day. What does that do for you?

*(Exit Simon, stage right, down the aisle and out of the room.)*

11

# TAMAR OF JERUSALEM

**CHARACTER:** **Tamar of Jerusalem:** She can be a woman of any age, young or old; she is loud spoken, cheerful, something of a gossip. She is wearing a blouse with long sleeves, a floor-length cotton skirt (plain color or striped), a kerchief tied over her hair, and a plain white apron.

**PROPERTIES:** Her symbol is a picture of a rooster, about a foot high, mounted on sturdy cardboard. On the back of the picture is a sturdy loop of cord securely taped, and so placed that the rooster will stand straight when it is attached to the hook on the cross.
Tamar should not carry the picture with her when she enters. There should be a small table inconspicuously placed near the front of the stage on which the rooster symbol is placed until she needs it.

**SCENERY:** None needed.

---

*(Enter Tamar up the aisle, stage right to center stage.)*

**TAMAR:** My name is Tamar. There is no reason why you should know me; I am a very unimportant person. Up until a little while ago, I had a really good job as serving maid in the house of Caiaphas, the high priest himself. Many less fortunate girls envied me. But I don't work for the high priest any more — and I am not sorry.

*(She walks over to look at the cross; then returns to center stage.)*

I was on duty last spring, two nights before the Passover feast. I'm not likely to forget it. There was a trial, a very unusual night trial, with the full Sanhedrin, at the high priest's house. Just between us *(she looks furtively to left and to right)* it was more than unusual — it was illegal! Even I, a serving maid, knew that. But it was my job to keep the tables supplied, not to worry about the ethics of the situation. I could tell you plenty about what goes on behind the scenes at the temple, but it will be healthier for me if I hold my tongue.

*(Again she looks to left and to right, like someone who does not want to be overheard.)*

Anyway, the place was full of people that night. Pharisees and priests, soldiers, and lots of servants like me. The important people were all inside, in the hall of assembly, and the others were hanging around the courtyard in groups, most of them trying to get close to a fire. It was a chilly evening. I was pretty excited by all the unusual activity. I didn't know the first thing about the prisoner they had dragged in, except that he was young, not bad looking, and they'd been knocking him around. A Nazarene, somebody said.

We don't have all that much use for Nazarenes, or for any other Galileans, for that matter. We even have a saying where I come from: "Can any good thing come out of Nazareth?" It's sort of a joke. You can tell Galileans by their north country twang.

I didn't hear the prisoner speak. We servants were shooed out of the hall of assembly, and I wandered out into the courtyard with everybody else. But there was a man there who was unmistakably a Galilean from his talk. He was a big fellow in rough clothes, rubbing his hands together over the fire; and he kept looking around as if he were afraid somebody was after him.

14

I went up to him and said, "You were also with the Naza-rene Jesus." He jumped a foot, and began backing away, pro-testing that he didn't know what I was talking about. He was acting so guilty — you know, like somebody who has come to steal the silver, or something — that I followed him, and said, "Certainly you are one of them, for you are a Galilean. Your tongue gives you away."

Well, he began to sweat, sputter, and swear, finally shout-ing, "I don't even know this man you are talking about!" And that's when it happened. I'll never forget it, if I live to be one hundred.

As soon as the words were out of his mouth, there was a sudden hush — and into the silence, a rooster crowed.

*(She walks over to the prop table, and picks up the sym-bol of the rooster, and shows it to the audience.)*

It was a strange thing to hear, because the sky was still dark, but the effect on the man was even stranger. He clutched his throat as if somebody has stabbed him — or maybe, as if he wanted to take the words back. And just then, at that very moment, they led the prisoner Jesus out into the courtyard, bruised and bound. He only looked at the Galilean, not say-ing a single word, but the big fellow burst into wild weeping, and raced out of the place as if the devil himself was after him, which maybe he was.

Then the soldiers hustled Jesus out of there, and I never saw him again. They said the Romans gave him a trial, and took him out and crucified him. That's what they said. But it was old Caiaphas who made it happen, you can bet on that.

*(She glances at the cross, and moves closer to it.)*

I've learned a lot since that night. I've been trying to find out who this Jesus was, and why they were conducting that trial. The most surprising thing about it is that some people are saying that this Jesus isn't dead — that he's the Son of God, and alive again. All Jerusalem is buzzing with it. Caiaphas is fit to be tied, especially since the big Galilean, whose name turns out to be Peter, has been preaching all over the city about it. And he isn't afraid any more. He doesn't seem to be afraid of anything now.

Don't you think that's strange?

*(She holds up the rooster again.)*

I keep remembering the rooster — the one that crowed that night in the dark. Do you suppose the rooster had anything to do with it?

*(She looks at the rooster, puzzled, and shakes her head.)*

Maybe someday I'll know more, but every time I hear a rooster crow, I think of Jesus of Nazareth, on his way to death, and of Peter the Galilean, who denied him.

*(Tamar places the rooster symbol on the cross, and exits stage right and down the aisle.)*

# ZIMRI THE PHARISEE

**CHARACTER:** **Zimri the Pharisee:** He is middle-aged, or made to look middle-aged. His bearing is proud and arrogant. He can be bearded. His dress is rich and somewhat ostentatious; gold or green tunic, belted; mantle of gold or green, long-sleeved and loose. He can wear gold or silver chains around his neck.

**PROPERTIES:** Zimri carries the scourge with him onto the stage. He demonstrates it to the audience, first showing how it is made, and then whipping it viciously through the air, as though he wished he had someone to use it on.

**SCENERY:** None needed. A simple curtain across the back of the stage is effective.

---

*(Enter Zimri, arrogantly, striding down the center aisle via stage right to center stage.)*

**ZIMRI:** My name is Zimri, son of Malchus, son of Shemiah; I am a Pharisee, and proud of it. We Pharisees have been the spiritual backbone of Israel for nearly 400 years. I want to be sure you understand that.
*(He holds up the scourge)*
See this? This is a scourge. Have you ever seen a scourge before?

*(He comes to the very edge of the stage, pointing to the different parts of the scourge as he describes it.)*

It is like a whip, you see, except for two things. It has many leather thongs to whip with instead of just one; and tied into the thongs are these sharp pieces of metal.

*(He walks up and down the stage, demonstrating the whipping action.)*

When a man is whipped with this thing, it doesn't just make lash marks on his back — it actually tears the flesh away from the bones. Men have dropped dead after being scourged forty times. So we have a penalty that calls for forty lashes minus one. That's supposed to leave a man alive, though I grant you, in the shape most of them are in at that point, they might prefer to take one more stroke, and die.

*(He lays the scourge down on the prop table and returns to center stage, standing defiantly with legs apart and arms folded.)*

I was there when the scourge was used on Jesus of Nazareth. My fellow Pharisees and I were among those who were demanding his crucifixion. When Pilate had him scourged, in an effort to appease us, I remember that I watched with approval. It satisfied something savage in me that day. I felt as if I was getting even.

*(He paces back and forth, center stage.)*

You see, every time we had had an encounter with that man, we had come out second best. He had scourged us more than once with his words. "Hypocrites," he called us — and "vipers" — and worst of all, he said we were "whitewashed tombs, full of dead men's bones and all uncleanness." He said that to **us** *(he shakes his fist)* — to us Pharisees, who pride ourselves on the cleanness and uprightness and correctness of our lifestyles! And somehow, he acted as if **he** was the one who had been deeply offended by **us**, instead of the other way around.

He ridiculed us before the crowds with transparent little stories he called parables, which portrayed us as stiff, unloving, self-righteous fools. Not only did we find that infuriating

18

— we felt it was dangerous. The whole structure of our temple worship was at stake, not to mention our standing with the people. Clearly, Jesus of Nazareth was a threat to our security, and he had to be disposed of.

*(He walks over and looks at the cross; then he returns to center stage. He is no longer angry; he speaks almost reluctantly, like a man confessing a crime.)*

But just between us, now that it's over, I don't feel as good as I thought I would. For one thing, there's that eerie business of the curtain in the temple inner chamber. The day Jesus was crucified, the curtain was found torn from top to bottom — yet the guards swore that no one had entered.

For another thing, I'm not proud of the way the trial was conducted. Trumped-up charges — falsified evidence — no defense witnesses called — an illegally-conducted trial from start to finish. It was the shabbiest sort of behavior for men like us, who consider ourselves righteous. When I meet my fellow Pharisees now, they don't look me in the eye, and they don't want to stop and talk. We broke all our own rules of justice. All of us are having trouble forgetting that.

*(He paces up and down, restlessly.)*

And then there's something else that keeps nagging at me, no matter how many times I try to get rid of it. The man did do some remarkable things. Do you suppose there is any slight possibility that he **was** the Messiah? That he really was who he said he was?

*(He pauses, looking thoughtful, chin in hand. Then he shakes himself out of it.)*

No, no — he wasn't, of course! We would have been the first to know.

*(Again he pauses, looking thoughtful, almost fearful.)*

But all those wild rumors that are racing around the city, about his coming to life again — suppose they should be true? What would that make us? What would it make **me**?

*(He looks apprehensively at the cross; then he picks up the scourge from the prop table, walks over to the cross and hangs it up, then exits stage right, dejectedly, in marked contrast to the way he came in.)*

19

# KING HEROD

**CHARACTER:** **King Herod:** Middle aged, richly dressed in colors of purple and gold, with a band of gold around his head. He is not a stable character; he is fretful, peevish, compaining; but he is also cruel and dangerous. He is also an ailing man with a bad stomach.

**PROPERTIES:** The purple robe and crown of thorns should be on the prop table so that he can pick them up as needed.

**SCENERY:** None needed.

---

*(Enter Herod, down the aisle via stage right to center stage, walking with pride, but not too fast.)*

**HEROD:** *(Proudly)* I am Herod. I come from a long line of Herods, and I am the King of the Jews.
*(His pride wilts a little; he speaks more confidentially.)*
Well, no — not really. I am only the Tetrarch of Galilee, and not ruler of all Israel. But I would **like** to be King of the Jews, although they hate me, and mutter about me behind my back. I am continuing to rebuild their temple for them — magnificently — they ought to be grateful. And yet they consider **me** unfit to worship in it!
*(He paces up and down, restlessly.)*
I am a man with power, at least in Galilee, but I am not a happy man. I am haunted by dreadful dreams, in which I

21

am pursued by a headless, bleeding prophet named John the Baptist. *(In a complaining voice)* And that doesn't strike me as fair, either. I didn't want to kill John. I was tricked into it by that witch, Salome. Why doesn't John haunt **her**? And now, since this business with Jesus of Nazareth, my stomach revolts at food, and there is a gnawing pain in my belly. *(He clutches his stomach as if in pain.)*

What **was** it about the man Jesus? I couldn't understand him. *(He shakes his head.)* When they first dragged him before me, I was glad, for I have heard of marvelous miracles done by him out in the rural areas. I believe in miracles — I think they are exciting. I would have been glad to see Jesus perform for me, and it would have been easy to reward a good performance with mercy.

But he would not even speak to me. That made me angry. Wouldn't you have been angry? I had the soldiers beat him, and abuse him; some of them even spit on him, but he still wouldn't respond.

Then I brought out a purple robe.

*(He walks over to the prop table, and picks up the purple robe.)*

It was **this** robe — and I told the soldiers that if the man thought he was royal, he should be dressed like royalty. They put it on him, and knelt to him in mock homage, and amused themselves for a long time. When we sent him back to Pilate, Pilate's soldiers even added this crown of thorn branches *(he picks up and shows the crown of thorns)* — which they jammed down on his head — and a reed for a sceptre which they put into his hand.

*(He pauses a moment, looking at the crown and robe.)*

But you know, that part of it was a mistake. The thing that chilled me, that haunts me still, is the memory of him standing there before me, dressed in the royal purple. Even though his hands were bound, and his face all swollen and bruised, that purple robe sat on him more naturally than it has ever sat on me.

Just for that one moment, I felt deep in my soul that I had no real right to be King of the Jews; but that **he** had a right to be king of everything — because that is what he was.

*(He walks over to the cross and puts the crown of thorns and the purple robe on the cross, and looks at them for a moment; then he shrugs his shoulders and turns back to center stage.)*

The moment passed, of course. I did not get to be where I am by being weak and sentimental. I reminded myself that the man was a problem. I know what to do with problems; unload them onto somebody else. I sent him back to Pilate, and Pilate disposed of him. Pilate's problem, not mine. And he's dead.

*(Suddenly, shrilly, clutching his hair with both hands)*

So why can't I sleep? Why can't I eat?

*(Herod hurries off stage right and down the aisle, looking apprehensively over his shoulder once, as if afraid somebody is coming after him.)*

# PILATE AND CLAUDIA

**CHARACTER:** **Pilate:** Middle aged; aristocratic appearance. He may be governor of Rome, but in this skit, he is a man having an argument with his strong-minded wife. He wears a Roman tunic, belted, of some rich material, preferably red, and sandals; also a cloak, thrown back over one shoulder.

**CHARACTER:** **Claudia:** Attractive, intelligent, vigorous woman. She is wearing a floor-length, softly draped gown, Grecian style, with one bare shoulder. (No sleeves)

**PROPERTIES:** A metal basin (silver, steel, or aluminum) should be on the prop table, with a pitcher beside it.

**SCENERY:** None needed.

---

*(Pilate and Claudia come rapidly down the aisle, Claudia in the lead, obviously angry, and Pilate trying to talk to her, trying to get her to stop. Even while they are going down the aisle he is calling "Claudia! Please wait!" When Claudia arrives at center stage via stage right, she turns to face him.)*

**PILATE:** I **tried** to release the man! The gods know I tried!

**CLAUDIA:** *(scornfully)* **You tried!** Are you Pontius Pilate, the Roman governor, or are you the garbage collector?

**PILATE:** Claudia, you weren't even there. You don't know how it was. If I could have let him go, I would have. I would have enjoyed doing it just to spite those weasels at the temple. Anybody would see with half an eye that the man was innocent, and that the charges against him had been trumped up out of hatred, or jealousy, or some such thing.

But there was the mob to worry about. They were the usual rabble, whipped to a frenzy by the agitators hired by the temple priests — but it was still a mob, totally out of control. I had to take that into consideration.

**CLAUDIA:** *(bitterly)* I wasn't expecting a simple act of mercy. There's no mercy **in** you. I know how many poor Jews you've condemned to the cross! And it wasn't even just because Jesus was falsely accused. It was the quality of the man himself. Couldn't you **see** it? Couldn't you **feel** it? If ever a man deserved a throne, and not a cross, it was that man, Jesus of Nazareth.

**PILATE:** I'll admit he was unusual. His eyes disturbed me. I was the governor, and he was the accused, yet somehow he seemed to be completely in control of the situation. There was no begging for mercy — he wouldn't even defend himself. It was all I could do to get him to talk to me at all. When I told him I was in a position to sentence him to death, he replied as cool as you please that I wouldn't have any power over him at all if it hadn't been given to me from above. What do you make of that?

**CLAUDIA:** That's no surprise to me. That's the kind of thing he's been saying about himself right along. I've seen him — I've listened to him speak. And I'm telling you, Pontius — you've done a very dangerous thing! The man wasn't just a man — he was godlike! I **tried** to warn you!

**PILATE:** Well, godlike or not, it's over. He's dead.

**CLAUDIA:** I wouldn't count on it.

**PILATE:** *(agitated)* Now, don't start that! Why do you want to say things like that?

**CLAUDIA:** I told you why. I wrote you that note. I had a dream about him, a terrifying dream, a dream of warning. But you wouldn't pay any attention.

**PILATE:** Now listen, Claudia, try to understand my situation. I'll tell you how it was, and you'll see I had no choice.

You know what Caesar said, the last time that the Jews rioted in Jerusalem — that if I couldn't keep order here, he'd find somebody who could. One more unsavory incident, and it's curtains for me. Have you any idea what the job opportunities are for a deposed Roman governor who's been stripped of his rank? I'd be lucky to find myself supervising the palace laundry! "Jesus claimed to be a king," they said. "If you let him go, you are not Caesar's friend," they said. I don't have to tell you how that would sound in Rome.

So I had him scourged, to try to pacify them. But they weren't satisfied with that. Then I tried to have him released, in accordance with the Passover custom of releasing one captive, to demonstrate mercy; but the crowd chose that murderer, Barabbas, instead.

What was a man to do? *(He throws up his hands)* Now listen, Claudia, because this was really clever.

*(He walks over to the prop table.)*

I called for this basin *(he sets it in front of him)* with water in it *(he pours water into basin from pitcher)*, and I put blame for his death right back on the people who were forcing me into this thing. I washed my hands clean, while they watched. I told them, "I am innocent of this man's blood. See to it yourselves." Wasn't that clever? They understood, Claudia — they shouted back, "Let his blood be upon us, and on our children!" So you see? It isn't my problem, not any more. It's **their** problem.

**CLAUDIA:** *(unmoved)* It's not that easy to wash blood off your hands, Pontius. You'll find out. The sight of it may disappear, but the stain of it, the feel of it, the memory of it, lasts forever. You sentenced Jesus of Nazareth to a criminal's death, and you think that's the end of it. What you have really done is to pass the sentence of eternal death upon yourself.

*(Exit Claudia, stage right and down the aisle. Pilate watches her go, shrugs his shoulders, then he picks up the basin, pours the water in it back into the pitcher, and hangs the empty basin on the cross. He stands back and looks at it for a moment, then exits stage right and down the aisle.)*

# THOMAS

**CHARACTER:** **Thomas:** He is an ordinary, honest looking man, bearded but not gray. He is dressed in a striped tunic, tied with a piece of rope, and a brown cloak.

**PROPERTIES:** Three railroad spikes and a small mallet are placed on the prop table.

**SCENERY:** None needed.

---

*(Thomas enters down the aisle via right stage to center stage. He projects determination, earnestness and honesty, but there is no arrogance in him. He is an ordinary, hard-to-convince nice guy.)*

**THOMAS:** My name is Thomas, and I am a disciple of Jesus. I'm not one of the important disciples, like Peter. I'm one of those whose names you may have trouble remembering. But when you do remember me, you probably think of a man who had to have things proved. I think it's only fair to let me tell my side of the story.
*(He walks over and looks at the cross; then returns to center stage.)*
Nobody loved Jesus more than I did. But I also have to say that probably none of the other disciples had a harder time than I did understanding the things Jesus said. When we asked him a question, he answered with another question or with

a story, or with a perplexing statement that we simply couldn't understand. At least, I couldn't. Maybe sometimes it was because we didn't want to understand.

*(He scratches his head, looking perplexed.)*

Looking back now, I can see that he tried to tell us many times that he was going to be put to death and rise again. But we never expected it to happen.

We were all there at the last supper before he died. He talked to us about many things. I knew that he was trying to prepare us for something terrible, something we all instinctively shrank from.

We were all there later, too, when he was arrested. We have been severely criticized for running away — but think about it a minute from our point of view.

The dinner had been very different from the usual Passover feast. We had been overwhelmed with sadness by Jesus' announcement that he was leaving us, although we still didn't grasp its full implications. Our heads were filled with his last discourses to us, some of his most profound teaching.

Then, in the garden of Gethsemane, when he was praying, we were shaken by Jesus' obvious distress. He was a man in deep grief. We had never seen him like that. The garden was a quiet place, and while he went some distance away to pray, most of us rolled up in our mantles and drifted off to sleep.

You can imagine the shock of being wakened by a mob of soldiers with torches, led by Judas — our friend, our companion, who had betrayed all of us to the authorities! Peter and I had swords, and began a feeble sort of defense; Peter actually cut a man's ear off with his. But Jesus promptly told us to put away our swords. He even healed the wounded ear. When the soldiers moved to arrest him, he simply gave himself over to them with the stipulation that they were to let us go.

What was a man to do? He didn't want us to stay with him, and he didn't want us to fight. We couldn't think of anything else to do, so we ran — ran like rabbits, all of us, except we found out later that Peter and John had followed Jesus at a distance.

I was there in the crowd the day Jesus was crucified. Most of us were, but spread out, one here, one there, trying not to attract attention. We didn't want to see it, but we couldn't stay away.

*(Thomas walks over to the prop table and picks up the three railroad spikes.)*

Have you ever seen a man crucified? I hope you never do. They put the cross on the ground, and laid Jesus on top of it. Then they placed his hands on the crossbeam — those wonderful hands of his, hands that had healed, comforted, and blessed, but had never hurt a single living thing — and they pounded huge nails through them. Nails like these.

*(He holds the nails up.)*

Have you ever had your hands punctured, even by something as thin as a needle? If you have, you know how it hurts. I leave you to imagine what it was like, not just to have these pounded through your hands, but to be hung up by them and left to die, with a jeering mob looking on.

*(He walks to the prop table, takes the mallet, and goes over to the cross and pounds the stakes into the holes on the cross.)*

It was horrible for him; it was also the most awful day of my life. I stayed until Jesus had died. I was too far away to hear his words from the cross, but I saw the soldier plunge a spear into his side, and I knew he was gone. Then I left, in such a haze of grief it is hard to remember even where I went, or what I did.

Then Sunday came. I was not with the others. I didn't see them until Monday morning, and they told me some wild tale about having seen Jesus alive again. Now, I put it to you. If you had watched a man die an unforgettable death — if you were as sure of that death as you were of your own name — what's your reaction going to be when somebody tells you he has been seen again, alive and well?

It was beyond belief, and I said so. I told them: "Unless I see in his hands the print of the nails, and place my finger in the mark of the nails, I will not believe!"

31

They were angry with me for not believing them. But they didn't believe, either, when the women first told them Jesus had risen! **They** didn't believe until they saw him for themselves. Why was I so terrible for wanting to see for myself?

*(Agitated, he runs his hands through his hair, and walks across the stage and back.)*

It was a whole week before I saw him. We were together in the upper room with the doors locked for safety, and suddenly Jesus was there. One minute he wasn't, and the next minute he was. It took my breath away. He walked right up to me and said, "Here, Thomas, put your fingers in the nail wounds, and be not faithless, but believing." And I sank to my knees, sobbing like a child, "My Lord and my God!"

*(Visibly moved, he pauses for a moment.)*

But he was very gentle. He put one of those poor, wounded hands on my head, and said softly, "Have you believed because you have seen, Thomas? Blessed are those who have not seen, and yet believe."

Well, I was never the same again after that night. You may call me slow to believe, but once I **do** believe, I'll stake my life on that belief. That, after all, is what we are asked to do.

What does it take to make **you** believe? Do you have to see miracles? Have visions? Hear voices? Take it from me — you have all you need in the Scriptures, all the evidence anyone should required. Give yourself to it, and believe. If you can believe, having **not** seen, you will draw down a blessing upon yourself, a personal blessing from Jesus, who was — and IS — the Son of God.

*(Exit Thomas, stage right, down the aisle out of the room.)*

# CENTURION

**CHARACTER:** **Centurion:** A man of military bearing, not too young, clean shaven. His costume is a real challenge, especially the helmet; it is worthwhile to investigate a theater supply company in your area. They could probably supply helmet and a short sword for less than $20. He wears a short tunic, preferably bright red; a breast plate (use silver cloth) and a wide belt with short sword attached. He has a short cloak fastened at one shoulder, and sandals. Greaves, or leg armor (shin guards) can be made out of foil covered cardboard. (optional)

**PROPERTIES:** A weathered sign, about 15 inches by 7 inches, with three rows of undecipherable printing.

**SCENERY:** None needed.

---

*(Enter Centurion down the aisle and up stage right to center stage. He is carrying weathered sign with three rows of lettering.)*

**CENTURION:** See this wooden sign? Know what it says? It says "King of the Jews" three times, in three different languages, so that nobody who could read at all could miss it.

When a man is crucified, he's intended to be an example to the people of what happens to wicked men who break the law. If a man is a murderer, for example, there will be a sign over his head saying "murderer," nailed to the cross on which he dies.

In the case of this Jesus from Nazareth, condemned to death by Pontius Pilate, there wasn't any reason for his death, except that the Sanhedrin demanded it, and had forced Pilate into a corner where he felt he had to give in. Pilate's only gesture of defiance was to insist on this sign to be nailed over the head of Jesus. He wrote the words himself. The temple authorities were furious — they tried to make him change the words to read "He claimed to be King of the Jews," but Pilate would only answer, "What I have written I have written." He handed it to me, and I nailed it up over Jesus' head myself. "King of the Jews" — hanging on a cross.

*(He takes the sign over to the cross and stands it up on the ledge of the crossbeam behind the two standing nails. He moves back a pace or two and looks at the cross; then returns to center stage.)*

It was a revolting spectacle. A crucifixion is no picnic, even when a man deserves that kind of death. But this one really turned my stomach. There were all the temple priests, shouting insults at him, so full of hate they fairly spat out the words. There was the crowd, as always, drawn by the sight and smell of the blood. And we soldiers were no better. We were the ones who had nailed him up there. It seemed as if the only decent person in the place was the man on the cross — the man who could look down as he was dying that terrible death and choke out the words, "Father, forgive them, for they know not what they do."

*(He pauses, walks back and forth for a moment.)*

Now, I've never been a superstitious man. But I stood beside the cross as this man died, and I heard him cry out, "Father, into thy hands I commit my spirit." As he slumped down limp and lifeless on the cross, the storm that had been building in the sky broke over our heads in fury. The ground shook. The sky seemed to split apart as the lightning tore it open. The rain poured down in torrents. It was as though an angry God was hurling all the weapons of the sky at us — at all of us — for what we had done.

I remember I looked up at him once more, before we raced for shelter —

*(He looks up at the cross)*

and the words burst out of me — "Surely this man was the Son of God!" I learned afterwards that the veil of the Jewish temple was torn in two, ripped from top to bottom by the earthquake. I'd like to hear old Caiaphas trying to explain that one away.

You know something? I haven't changed my mind. I've been on my knees every night since, praying that the God whose son Jesus was willing to die for me, would forgive me for what I have done. I believe he was — I believe he **is** the Son of God.

Who do **you** believe he is — Jesus of Nazareth?

*(He looks once more toward the cross and exits, stage right and down the aisle out of the room.)*

# PALM SUNDAY YOUTH ONE-ACT

*(NOTE: The two actors are teenagers, but either boys or girls. I have used the names Jamin and Azor, but they might just as well be Judith and Deborah, or Jamin and Judith.)*

*(Enter Azor, walking across stage left toward stage right. Jamin comes down center aisle at a run, calling to Azor.)*

**JAMIN:** Azor, wait for me!

*(Azor turns toward the voice, and obediently stops walking. Jamin joins him, center stage.)*

**JAMIN:** Did you see the procession? Did you see Jesus? Wasn't it **great**?

**AZOR:** I saw some sort of parade, all right, and somebody sitting on a donkey, and people throwing branches and clothes under the feet of the donkey. There was a lot of shouting, but I didn't know what it was all about.

**JAMIN:** It was the prophet, Jesus of Nazareth. And they were shouting because they believe he is the Messiah, come to set his people free.

**AZOR:** Why should they think that? He looked pretty ordinary to me.

**JAMIN:** My father says there's a prophecy in Zechariah, about the king coming into Jerusalem seated on the colt of a donkey.

**AZOR:** O come on, Jamin! This isn't the first time anybody's come to the city riding a donkey!

**JAMIN:** Of course not — but it's important because it's **this** man riding on a donkey. A whole lot of people have heard Jesus teach, and have seen him do miracles. Some of us were in Bethany a couple of weeks ago, when he did the greatest thing of all.

**AZOR:** You were there? What did he do?

**JAMIN:** He brought back to life a man who had been dead four days.

**AZOR:** Come on, I don't believe that. It's impossible. It must have been some kind of trick. The guy probably wasn't dead at all.

**JAMIN:** He was good and dead. They'd performed all the burial rites, and wrapped him in burial clothes, and sealed him in a tomb in the rock. The hired mourners were there and the whole town had turned out. He was a very popular man.

**AZOR:** And you actually saw this — this thing happen? What did this Jesus do?

**JAMIN:** Jesus had been a good friend of Lazarus and his sisters, and he went with them to the tomb. They were all weeping; but Jesus stepped forward and said, "Take away the stone!"

**AZOR:** But if the man had been dead four days — the body would have already started to decay! There would have been a terrible smell!

**JAMIN:** That's what the man's sister Martha said. But Jesus answered, "Didn't I tell you that if you would believe, you would see the glory of God?" Nobody could answer that, so they took away the stone. Then Jesus prayed, real loud so all the people could hear him; and then he shouted, "Lazarus, come out!" It was so scary, Azor! Some of the women fainted away. But suddenly, the dead man appeared in the door of the tomb, still wrapped in the burial bandages — like a walking mummy! And Jesus said, "Unbind him, and let him go." And they did! He was white and thin — you could tell he'd been really sick — but he was alive again. I tell you, it was wonderful!

**AZOR:** Well, I guess! I wish I'd been there. I can see why you would think Jesus is the Messiah. Who else could do things like that? Was the crowd impressed?

**JAMIN:** A lot of them believed in him on the spot. But some of the Pharisees looked pretty sour. And I don't think the priests in the temple are pleased. They don't want to believe in Jesus because he's said some pretty sharp things about them.

**AZOR:** Wow! I wish I'd known all this before I saw the procession. I'd have thrown branches and shouted too. What do you suppose is going to happen next?

**JAMIN:** I don't know, but I'm sure going to find out. My father loaned Jesus the donkey he's riding, and I'm supposed to bring it home again when he's through with it. Do you want to go to the city with me, and see what's happening?

**AZOR:** I wouldn't miss it for anything!

*(Exit the two boys, briskly walking or running down the center aisle.)*

# MAUNDY THURSDAY
Meditation for a pastor to accompany communion

Here on the cross before you are symbols of the Easter story — the ageless, dramatic, true account of the full extent to which God, and the Son of God, were willing to go for love of their people. They are tragic symbols — symbols of betrayal, of denial, of mockery, of cruel torture, of death.

Tonight, for the first time in the story, our symbols are a little different. For the first time, we are given a whisper of hope as the purpose behind the tragedy is revealed. Jesus made it very clear that he intended us as well as the disciples to understand that purpose, and to commemorate the event that fulfilled it. The symbols he has given us are the bread and the cup.

*(He holds up the bread and cup.)*

Let us try tonight to grasp the full meaning of them, and to enrich our understanding of this sacrament in which we, as well as the disciples, participate — in order that Easter this year may burst upon us with a newness of glory we have never experienced before.

In order to do this, we must go even farther back in time, beyond Maundy Thursday to the Passover itself. It was no accident that Jesus tied his communion meal to the Passover feast. His symbolic use of the bread and the cup of wine were not afterthoughts, hastily tacked onto a feast that was already rich with meaning for faithful Jews. Jesus' intent was to give the meaning of the Passover feast a whole new dimension. The event of the Last Supper is one of the most wonderful bridges between the Old Testament and the New Testament accounts. I imagine that the communion sacrament has a meaning for converted Jews, such as Jews for Jesus, that we can only dimly realize. But let us try.

41

The original Passover meal was commanded by God on the last night that the slave nation of Israel spent in the land of Egypt, back in the days of Moses. You will recall that Moses had been dispatched by God to Pharaoh of Egypt, with orders that he was to allow the captive Israelites to leave Egypt to return to their own land.

It isn't too difficult to understand why Pharaoh was reluctant to do this. The entire economy of his county revolved around the slave system. In Pharaoh's case, he drew down upon Egypt the wrath of God, in the form of a series of increasingly devastating plagues; yet in his stubborn heart he would not yield, in spite of the demonstrations of God's power and anger through Moses.

The last plague was the most terrible of all. Moses told Pharaoh that God was going to strike dead the first born of every household in Egypt, from the household of Pharaoh himself to that of the lowliest slave, even including the Egyptian cattle. The plague would fall at midnight, and the Israelites would be spared provided they were obedient in following all the things God told them to do. It was a series of symbolic actions, to help the people to remember through all their generations for all time what God did for them in Egypt.

This is what they had to do. First, each household was to slay a lamb, a pure and spotless lamb with no blemishes of any kind. They were to take a branch of hyssop, a bitter herb used medicinally as a purge, dip it into the blood of the lamb, and mark the doorposts of their houses with blood. The flesh of the lamb was to be roasted and served with unleavened bread and bitter herbs, and the people were to eat with their traveling clothes on, for the next day they would be leaving Egypt forever.

This was called the Passover Feast, because when the angel of death sent by God to smite the Egyptians saw the blood on the doorposts of the Israelite homes, he **passed over** and spared them.

When we look at the story of the Exodus with the eyes of enlightened Christians, its symbolism for us becomes clear. It was a real event, a true story; it is also deeply symbolic.

42

Just as the Israelites were in slavery to the Egyptians, so all people are in slavery to sin. Just as Moses delivered the Israelites who obeyed him, so Jesus Christ delivers the Christians who obey him. In Egypt, the blood of spotless lambs marked doors of those who were spared death from the wrath of God. Likewise, the blood of Christ, God's one spotless lamb, was shed to save all those who are "under the blood" — that is, those of us who follow Jesus in obedience, as the obedient Israelites followed Moses.

This is why, at the Passover feast in the upper room, Jesus made use of traditional elements of the meal, the bread of communion and the cup of communion. They are different from all the other symbols connected with the Easter event because in them, we actually participate in something. We cease to be spectators; we identify ourselves with faithful Christians of all ages — and even with God's faithful Jews of the Old Testament. By eating and drinking these elements as God has commanded, and by declaring anew our dedication of ourselves to his service, we draw close again to our Lord in obedience and grateful remembrance.

*(Pastor places symbols on the cross and proceeds with communion.)*

# MARY MAGDALENE
Easter Morning Monologue

*(The cross which has been on stage for all of the Lenten skits is still there, but all of the other symbols have been removed.)*

*(Enter Mary Magdalene, stage left. She crosses over to stage right, and lays one hand on the upright part of the cross. She has an Easter lily in one hand. [optional])*

**MARY:** It's empty now. And if you know about the horrible agony of the death that our Lord Jesus suffered on this cross, you have wept over it, as I have.

I have wept today too, but my tears are tears of joy. I bring you news — the most wonderful news in the world! The grave of Jesus is empty, too!

*(She walkes to center stage)*

You may find it hard to believe, but I have seen the Master with my own eyes, alive again and walking again on this earth. The disciples did not believe me; they thought I was hysterical with grief. But let me tell you what I have seen with my own eyes, just as it happened.

*(She walks back and forth for a moment, as if collecting her thoughts. Then she pauses again center stage.)*

As all the world must know by now, Jesus died two days ago, on Friday, the day before the Sabbath. We knew that Joseph of Arimathea had provided a tomb for him, and we marked the spot, for there was not enough time to anoint his body properly for burial before the Sabbath day. And of course, we could not do it on the Sabbath.

But we gathered and prepared spices, and this morning very early, before dawn, a group of us women went to the tomb. James' mother, Mary, was with us, and Salome and Joanna. As we walked, we asked one another how on earth we were going to deal with the huge stone which had been rolled in front of the tomb.

We knew that the temple guards had placed a watch of soldiers at the grave, and I was hoping they might be willing to help us, and to let us complete the burial preparations. After all, they were only there to see that no one stole the body. His enemies remembered he had said he would rise from the dead, and although they didn't believe it, they were afraid his disciples might steal the body, and pretend he had risen. Wasn't it strange that his enemies remembered that saying, and his friends had all forgotten it?

But as we walked, we felt the ground tremble beneath us; and when we reached the tomb, to our amazement we saw that the soldiers were gone, the stone was rolled away, and the grave was empty!

My first thought was to go fetch the disciples. I left the other women there and ran almost all the way to the place where Simon Peter and John were staying, and shouted to them, "They have taken the Lord out of the tomb, and we don't know where they have put him!"

Well, both of them went racing for the tomb. John got there first and waited for Peter, and together they went into the tomb and saw the burial clothes lying there like the chrysalis of a butterfly, empty. They puzzled and puzzled about it, but could throw no light on the situation, and finally they left. And none of us knew at that time what had become of the soldiers.

After Peter and John left, I stayed behind. I just couldn't bring myself to leave. The other women had gone also; I talked to them afterward and found that while I was fetching the disciples, they had seen angels who told them Jesus had risen from the dead. But at that moment, standing alone outside the tomb, I knew nothing of that. I knew only that the Master whom

I had loved so dearly had died, and that I was not even going to be able to perform this last loving service to his poor shattered body.

As I stood in the garden weeping, I looked once again into the empty tomb, and suddenly I saw two figures in white, seated at the head and foot of the place where the body of Jesus had lain. They spoke to me, saying, "Woman, why are you weeping?" and I answered, "They have taken my Lord away, and I don't know where they have put him."

Then I turned around and there was another figure standing behind me, between me and the sun. He also asked me why I was crying. I couldn't see his face, which was in shadow, and I thought it was the gardener, so I said, "Sir, if you have carried him away, tell me where you have put him, and I will get him."

*(She paces up and down for a moment.)*

And then — then he said just one word. He called my name — "Mary!" and I knew, I knew! "Rabboni!" I cried out, and I threw myself at his feet. I can't even begin to describe what it was like! He was alive, the same, yet not the same. There was a glory about him. He said to me,

"Do not hold on to me, for I have not yet returned to the Father. Go instead to my brothers and tell them, 'I am returning to my Father and your Father, to my God and your God.' "

Then when I looked up, he was gone as suddenly as he had come. Somehow that didn't surprise me at all. I was too full of joy at his return, too overwhelmed with the magnificence of it. Death had not been able to hold him! Death, to him, was no more than a door, through which he could come and go at will! And his words meant that for us, his disciples, death would lose its terrors, for it would be only a way for us to go where he had already gone before us.

I went as he had bidden me, and told the disciples what had happened. The other women had already told them about having seen the angels, but they didn't believe any of us. It's hard to blame them; I'm not sure I could have believed it if I had not seen it myself.

But **you** believe, don't you? You have our words, our witness, and we are telling the simple truth. Later the disciples believed, but not until they had seen him. But Jesus has said, "Blessed are those who have **not** seen, and yet believe." I invite you to that belief this morning. Gather in that blessing for yourselves; I promise you, your life will never be the same again!

*(Exit Mary, stage right. If she is carrying a lily [optional], she stops and places it on the cross, and then exits.)*

# CONSTRUCTION NOTES FOR BASE OF CROSS

**Materials:** 2 pieces of lumber 2 inches by 6 inches by 30 inches
4 pieces of lumber 2 inches by 6 inches by 12 inches
4 shelf brackets, L shaped, with both arms of the L at least 11 inches long

Assemble first
layer of base:

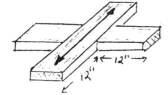

Assemble second
layer of base:

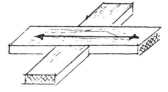

Place second layer on
top of first layer;
nail together.

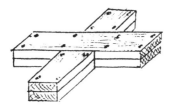

Screw shelf brackets to base, as shown. Brackets should enclose a space roughly 4-1/8 inches by 4-1/8 inches, into which bottom of cross can be inserted.

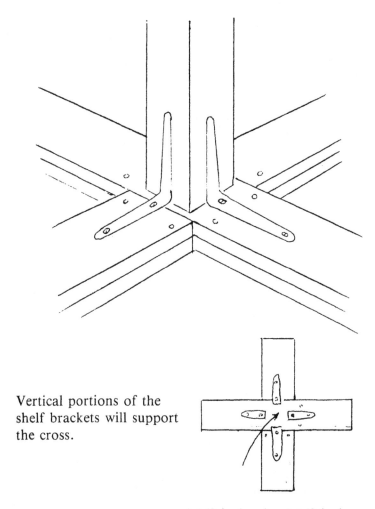

Vertical portions of the shelf brackets will support the cross.

4-1/8 inches by 4-1/8 inches space

# CONSTRUCTION NOTES FOR CROSS

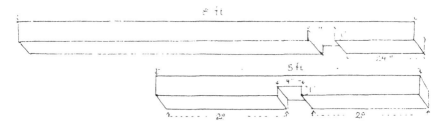

One 8-foot 4 inch by 4 inch
and one five-foot 4 inch by 4 inch
with 4 inch by 1 inch cutouts, as
shown.

Assemble as shown and nail in place.

Crosspiece will form
narrow ledge on which
sign "King of the
Jews" will rest.

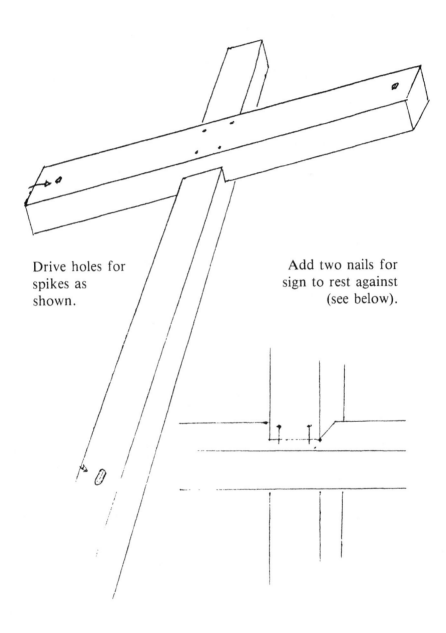

Drive holes for
spikes as
shown.

Add two nails for
sign to rest against
(see below).

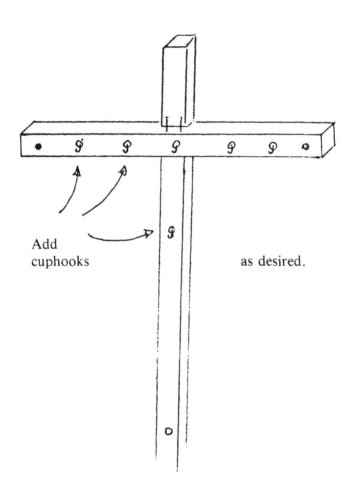

Add
cuphooks                                    as desired.

# CONSTRUCTION NOTES
# FOR SCOURGE

The **scourge** is a whip made with a short wooden handle and rawhide thongs secured at one end, into which bits of metal have been tied.

**Handle:** The turned leg of an old wooden chair is ideal. A 3/4-inch dowel can be used. One inch from the end of the handle, cut out a groove 1/8-inch deep and 1/2-inch wide. Handle is approximately 15-inches long.

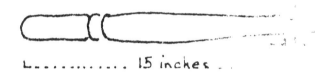

L............... 15 inches

**Thongs:** Two 48-inch-long pieces of rawhide, folded in half, with the folded section wound tightly around the cut-out portion of handle, and knotted in place.

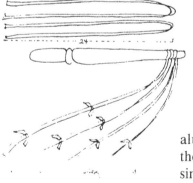

Twist small pieces of aluminum foil around thongs in various places to simulate scraps of metal.

CPSIA information can be obtained
at www.ICGtesting.com
Printed in the USA
BVOW09s1602070318
509943BV00028B/1495/P